EYE ILLUSIONS™

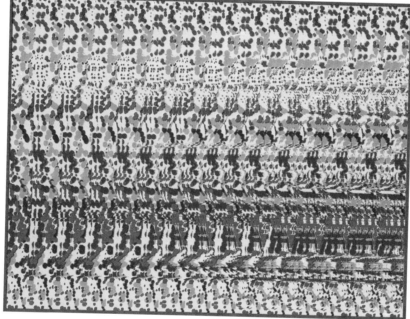

Written by Jim Anderson
Book Design by TXF Graphics

COPYRIGHT ©1994 Modern Publishing, a division of Unisystems, Inc.
TM Eye Illusions is a trademark of Modern Publishing, a division of Unisystems, Inc.
Distributed by Ladybird Books Ltd Loughborough Leicestershire UK
© LADYBIRD BOOKS LTD 1994, LADYBIRD and the device of a Ladybird are trademarks of Ladybird Books Ltd

INTRODUCTION

Welcome to a new world! Hidden within the beautiful abstract pictures in this book are exciting three-dimensional images. All you need to do is look at the pictures in a special way, relax, and the images will unfold in front of you as if by magic. You will see images of animals and toys, people and things – all in brilliant colour and sharp detail. You might even be tempted to reach out and touch them!

The wonderful images in this book are called 'stereograms'. They are flat, two-dimensional pictures that, when viewed in a certain way, appear to have three dimensions.

In three-dimensional – or 3-D pictures – things not only have height and width, they have depth as well.

Early 3-D pictures were really two images, and you needed special glasses or a special viewer to look at them. Thanks to modern computer technology, stereograms are now single images that can be viewed directly by anyone!

For hundreds of years scientists have been studying how vision works. Artists began using this knowledge to draw 3-D pictures over 150 years ago, but because they drew everything by hand, it took them ages to create even one image. The development of computers changed everything. Starting in the 1960s, artists used computer graphics to create ever more complex 3-D art. At first the 3-D images were simple shapes and designs. As computer graphic technology improved, and as the artists grew in their craft, more detailed and exciting pictures were created.

We can see these pictures in three dimensions because all human beings have 'binocular' vision. Our eyes are several centimetres apart, so each eye sees things from a slightly different angle. This information is combined in the brain to give us a 3-D view of the world. Stereograms, although they look like simple abstract patterns, actually contain all the information the brain needs to 'see' a 3-D image. The information for the right eye is on the right side of the picture, and that for the left eye is on the left side. By relaxing the focus of your eyes, you allow the two sides to overlap, and the brain is 'tricked' into seeing a 3-D picture. It's a simple idea made possible thanks to complex technology. These 3-D pictures really do show us a whole new world!

INSTRUCTIONS

To see these 3-D images you need the right setting. First, find a quiet place with bright lighting, and make sure the picture you look at is evenly lit. Then sit up straight, take a deep breath, and relax. This is very important. The more relaxed you are, the easier it will be to find the images, and the more fun you will have. Also, be patient, particularly at the beginning. It may take several minutes before you can see the picture in three dimensions. So take it easy and don't give up! There are several ways of viewing the 3-D images in this book:

Method One

Begin by looking at the cover picture. The cover is shiny, and you should be able to see your reflection, or the reflection of a light in it. Look at the picture on the cover, but focus your eyes on the reflection. This will make your eyes relax and go out of focus. Stare at the picture for a minute or two until you 'feel' something start to happen. Just relax, continue staring, and the 3-D image will appear.

Method Two

Another way to see the 3-D image is to bring the picture right up to your nose. Don't try to see the image – just let your eyes go completely out of focus. Then, while keeping your eyes out of focus, move the picture back to about arm's length. Keep looking at it with your eyes relaxed, and after a little while, the 3-D image will 'pop' out.

Method Three

A third approach is to try and 'see through' the picture. Look at the page, relax your eyes, and imagine you are looking 'beyond' the book. Keep looking for a few minutes. Remember, patience is important. So is relaxation. Just take it easy and enjoy yourself. In time a beautiful 3-D image will appear in front of you.

These three methods make up the 'parallel-viewing' technique. There is also a 'cross-eyed' technique that is more comfortable for some people.

Method Four

To view the images in the cross-eyed way, bring your finger, or a pen or pencil, up close to your eyes. Focus on the finger, pen or pencil. As you hold this focus look at the stereogram. It may take a few minutes but the 3-D image will appear.

Once you develop one technique try to develop another. Sometimes different techniques allow you to see slightly different images in the same stereogram. For example, if you look at a 3-D image of birds flying in the sky, the parallel-viewing technique may show you the birds in front, with the clouds in the background. With the cross-eyed technique, however, you may see the clouds in front, looking as if the birds have already flown through them leaving bird-shaped holes!

There are 14 images in this book each with a riddle to help you discover what they are. If you're patient and keep at it you will soon be able to see all of them. Then you will be a true expert in the world of 3-D!

Opposite: *What do you call a charging, snorting animal that's having a quick snooze! This is the name of a mighty machine that's always around when there's movement of ground.*

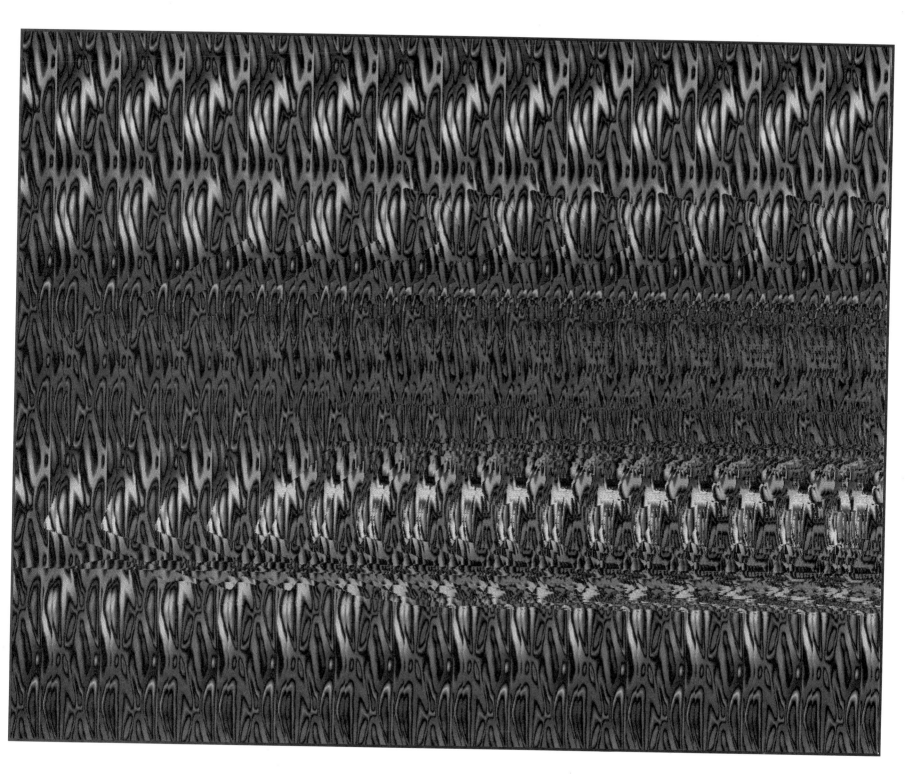

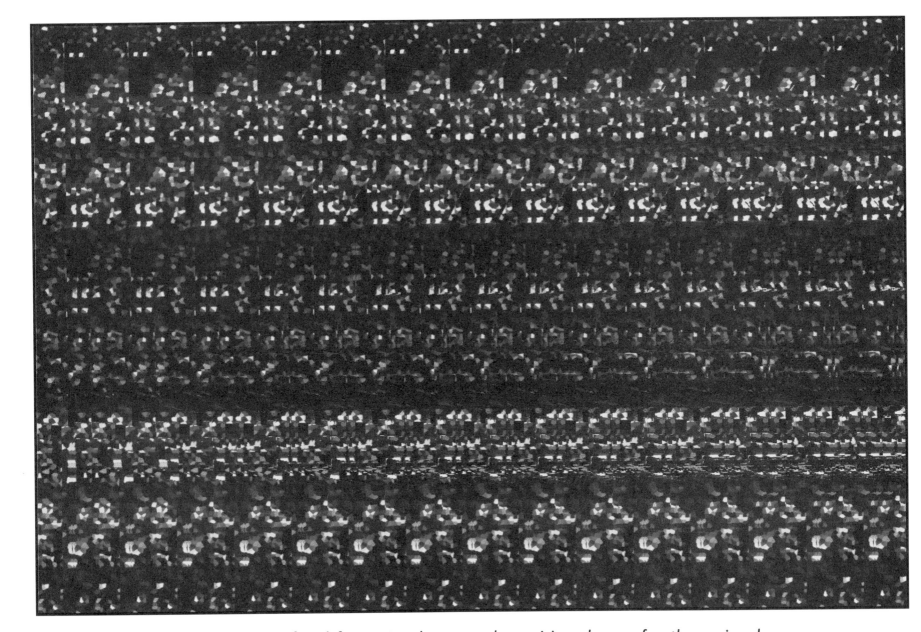

Farmers use this to store food for animals, or perhaps it's a home for the animals themselves!

You would be right to think of a pen, but you'd be wrong to think of writing. If someone says you're like one, they aren't being very kind!

Here's an animal doing Big Top tricks. He's large and furry, with big teeth and claws, but he's been trained to be friendly and enjoy the applause.

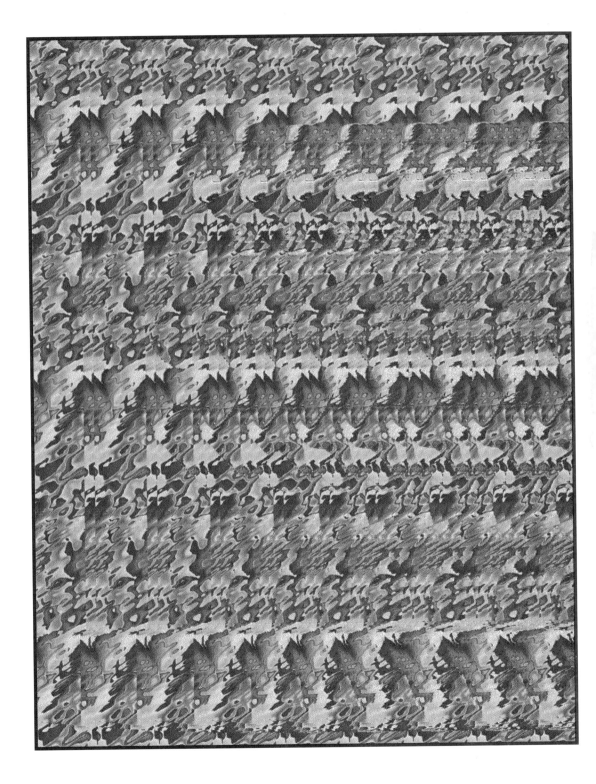

Hey presto! This is a
magician's favourite trick.
Can you see what's
appeared from his hat?

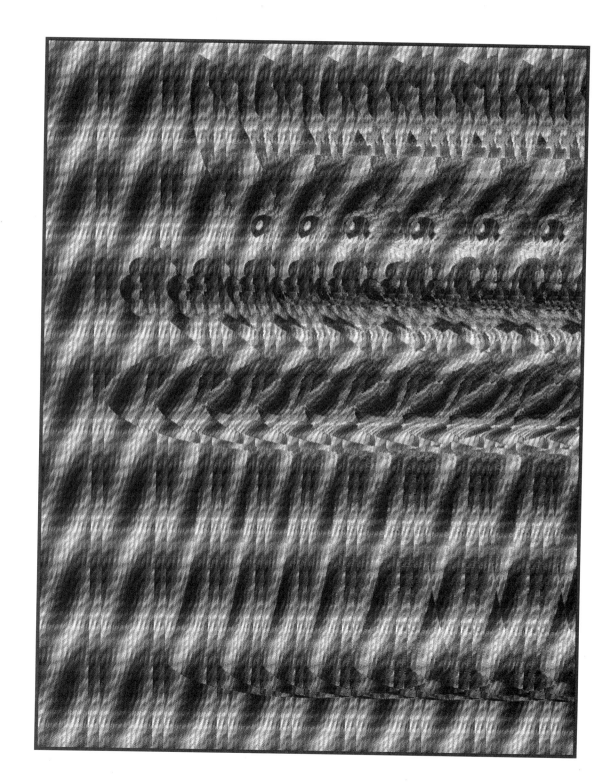

You can get a bird's eye view of things from this machine. You will land on the land, see the sea and be there in the air.

Opposite:
Big or small, fancy or simple, you'll find them in lots of houses, and they often have houses of their own.

Overleaf:
Marching soldiers say that these can't be beaten... but they are to make a sound!

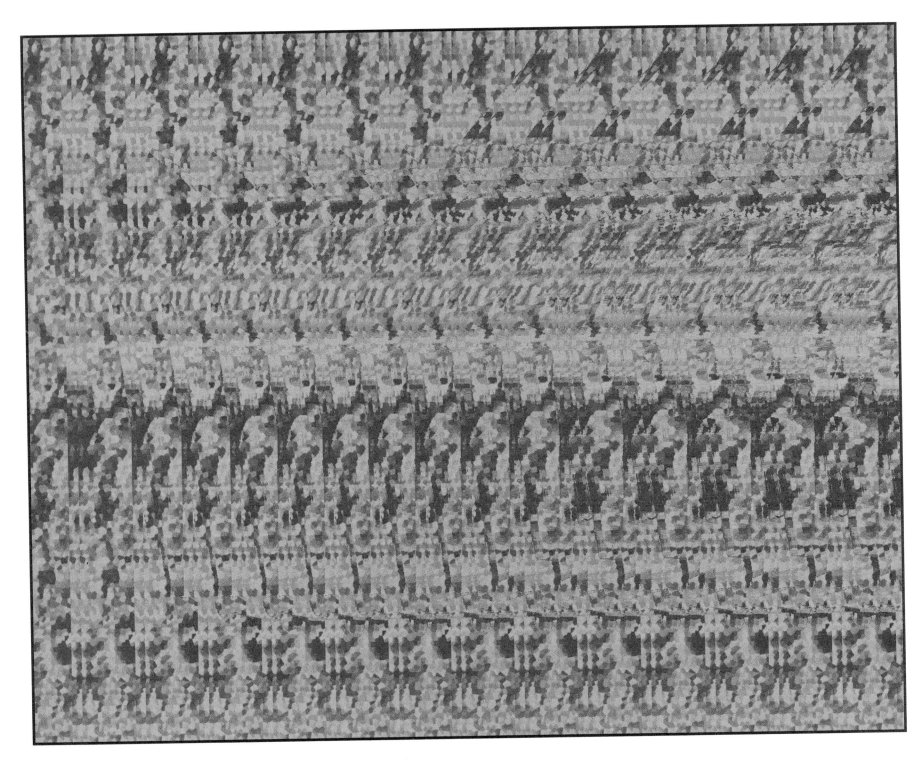

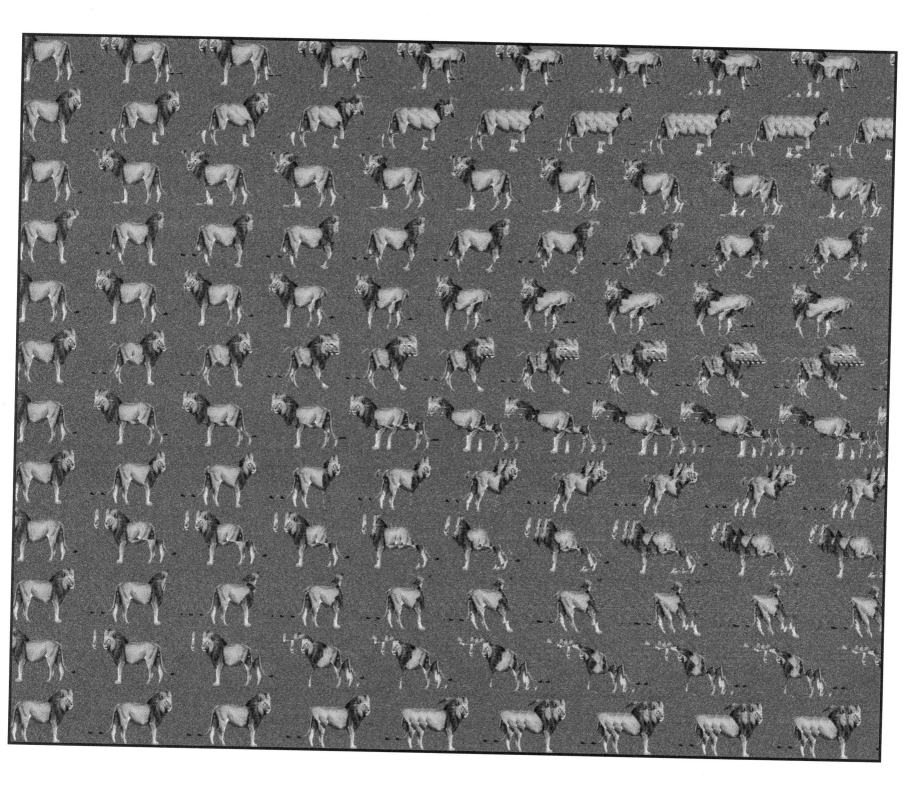

Previous page:
He's called the king, but he doesn't have a crown. The main thing he has around his head is fur.

Opposite:
Oh dear! It sounds like a creamy sweet, but it's a four-legged animal that puts its head first when fighting.

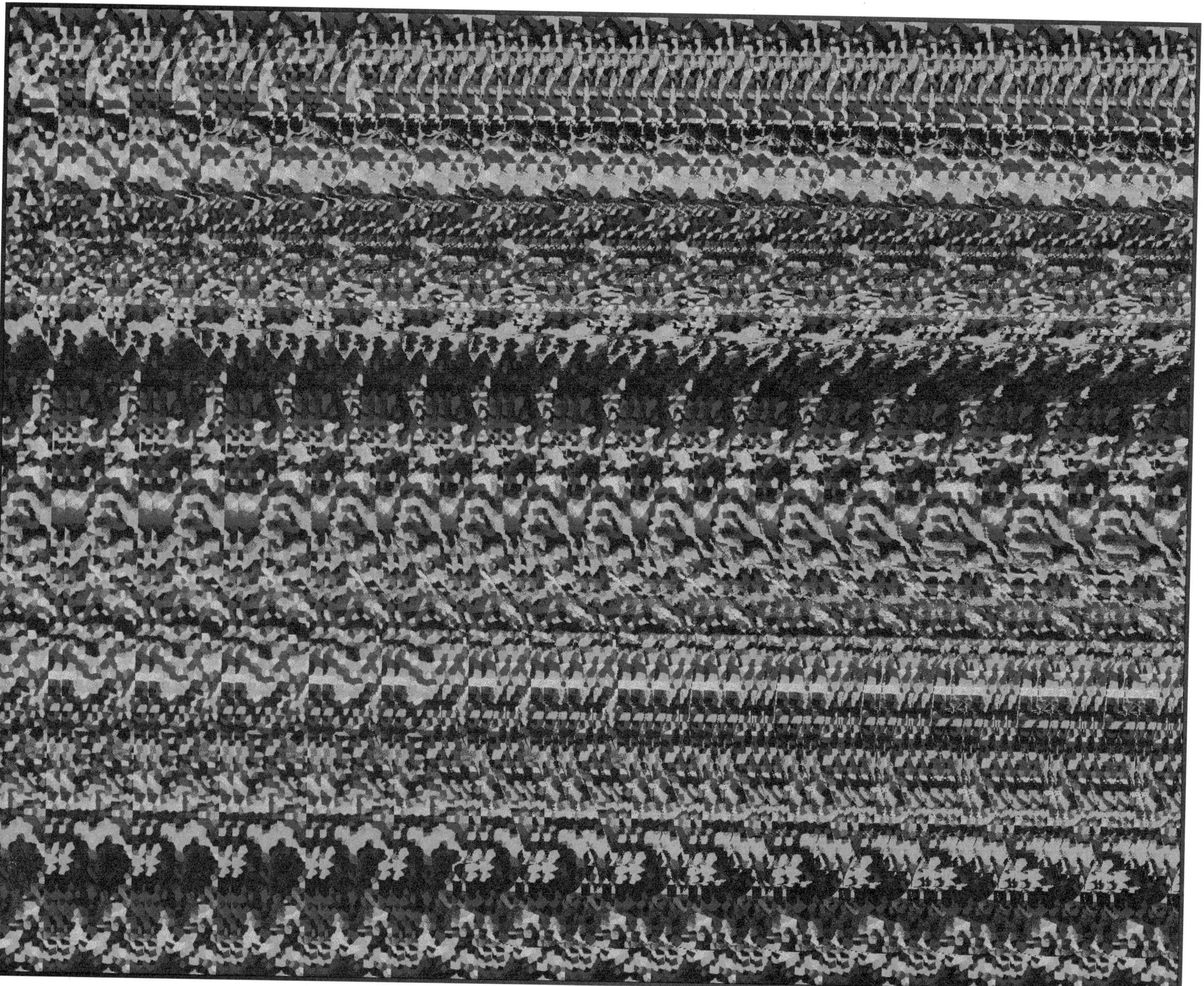

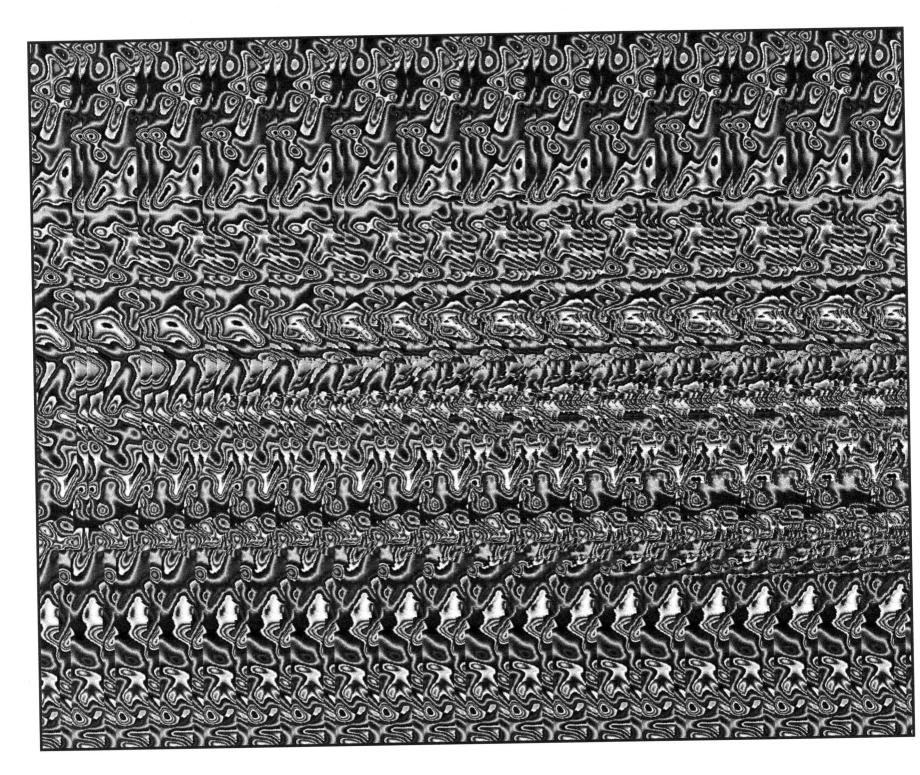

Opposite:

Toot! Toot! If you're lost at sea on a stormy night you'll be happy to hear that sound. This craft does all the hard work, and even though it's small, it can move big ships.

In the wild they can be grizzly, but when you find this at home it's soft and furry. Most of them are given names — like Edward.

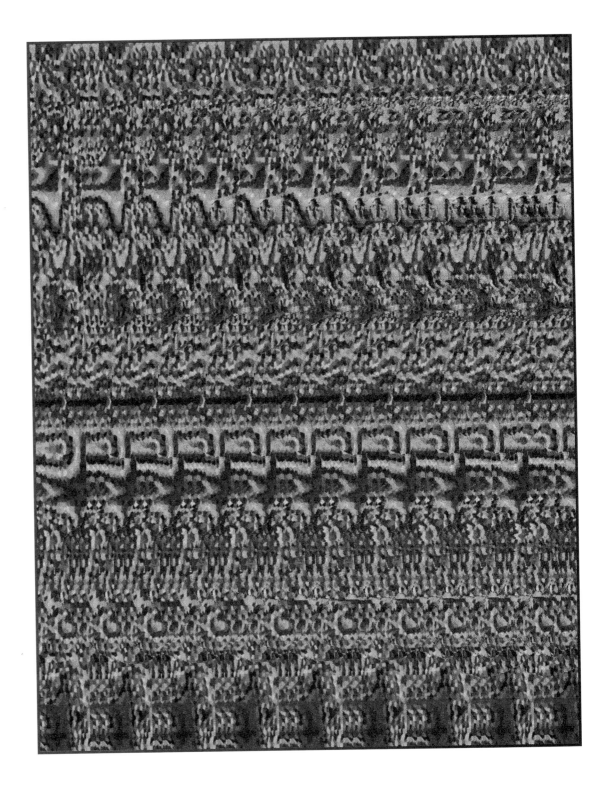

Here's a bright bird that likes to stick its nose into everything. Ask a friend to help if you're stuck. Two can solve it!

One of our favourites... and we're really glad he saw us!

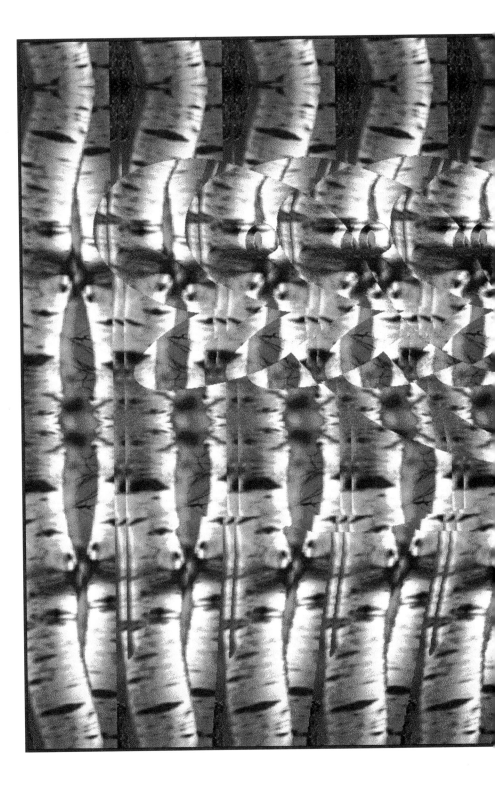

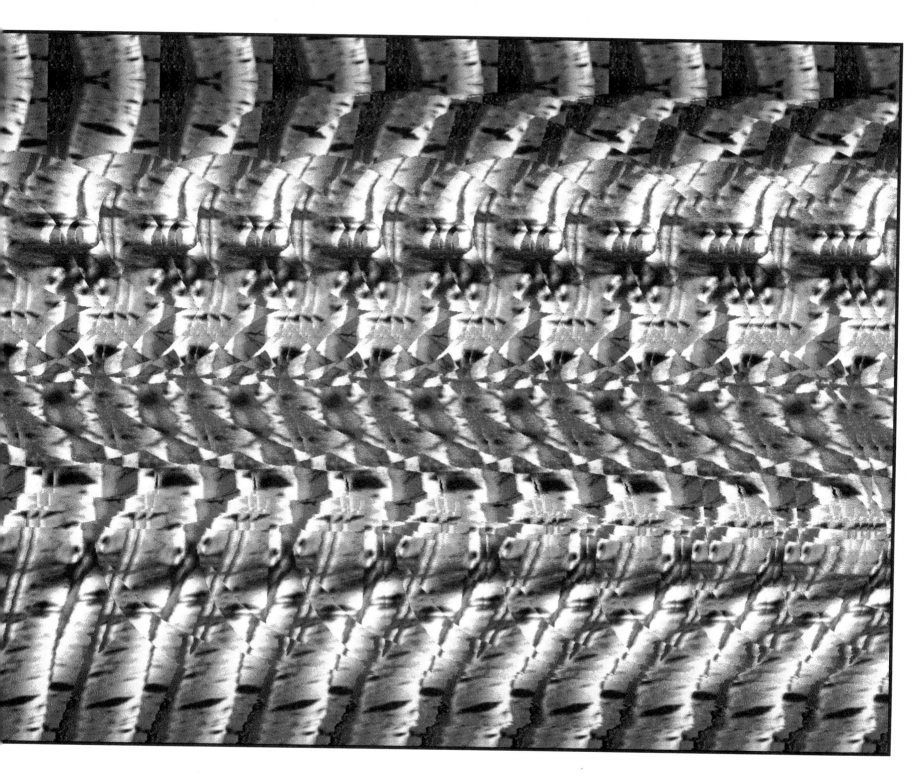

page 5   Bulldozer

page 6   Barn

page 7   Pig

page 8   Circus bear

page 9   Magician's rabbit

pages 10–11   Aeroplane

page 12   Dolls

page 14   Drums

page 15   Lion

page 17   Moose

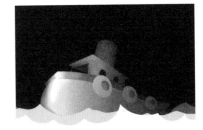

page 18   Tug boat

page 20   Teddy bear

page 21   Toucan

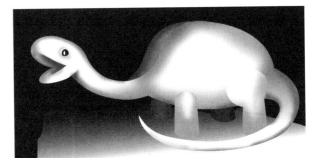

pages 22–23   Dinosaur